The Long Marriage

MAXINE AND VICTOR KUMIN WITH GUS AND CLAUDE (1978). *Kelly Wise*

MAXINE KUMIN

The Long Marriage

POEMS

W. W. NORTON & COMPANY

NEW YORK LONDON

For information about permission to reproduce selections from this book,
write to Permissions, W. W. Norton & Company, Inc., 500 Fifth Avenue,
New York, NY 10110

The text of this book is composed in Bembo with the display set in Centaur
Composition by Tom Ernst
Manufacturing by the Maple-Vail Book Manufacturing Group
Book design by Chris Welch
Production manager: Julia Druskin

Library of Congress Cataloging-in-Publication Data

Kumin, Maxine, date.

The long marriage : poems / Maxine Kumin.

p.   cm.

ISBN 0-393-04351-7

I. Title.

PS3521.U638 L63 2001

811'.54—dc21   2001034553

W. W. Norton & Company, Inc., 500 Fifth Avenue, New York, N.Y. 10110
www.wwnorton.com

W. W. Norton & Company Ltd., Castle House,
75/76 Wells Street, London W1T 3QT

1 2 3 4 5 6 7 8 9 0

For Victor, "on the dark lake . . ."

Contents

I

Skinnydipping with William Wordsworth

I lie by the pond *in utter nakedness*
thinking of you, Will, your epiphanies
of woodcock, raven, rills, and craggy steeps,
the solace that seductive nature bore,
and how in my late teens I came to you
with other Radcliffe *pagans suckled in*
a creed outworn, declaiming whole swatches
of "Intimations" to each other.

Moist-eyed with reverence, lying about
the common room, rising to recite
Great God! I'd rather be . . . How else
redeem the first flush of experience?
How else create it again and again? *Not in*
entire forgetfulness I raise up my boyfriend,
a Harvard man who could outquote me
in his Groton elocutionary style.

Groping to unhook my bra he swore
poetry could change the world for the better.
The War was on. Was I to let him die
unfulfilled? Soon afterward we parted.
Years later, he a decorated vet,

I a part-time professor, signed the same
guest book in the Lake District. Stunned
by coincidence we gingerly shared a room.

Ah, Will, high summer now; how many more
of these? *Fair seed-time had my soul,*
you sang; what seed-times still to come?
How I mistrust them, cheaters that will flame,
gutter and go out, like the scarlet tanager
who lights in the apple tree but will not stay.

Here at the pond, your *meadow, grove, and stream*
lodged in my head as tight as lily buds,
sun slants through translucent minnows, dragonflies
in paintbox colors couple in midair.
The fickle tanager flies over the tasseled field.
I lay my "Prelude" down under the willow.
My old gnarled body prepares to swim
to the other side.
                    Come with me, Will.
Let us cross over sleek as otters,
each of us bobbing in the old-fashioned breaststroke,
each of us centered in our beloved Vales.

Thinking of Gorki While Clearing a Trail

It wasn't exactly raining but
a little wetness still dribbled down.
I had been reading and sorrowing
and set out with the dogs as an antidote.
They went ahead snuffling in the leaf plaster.
Despite the steady snick of my clippers
boletus mushrooms kept popping soundlessly
out of the ground. How else account for
the ones with mouse-bites out of the caps
when I doubled back on my tracks?

The animals have different enzymes
from us. They can eat amanitas
we die of. The woodpeckers' fledglings
clack like a rattle of drumsticks each time
crumpled dragonflies arrive and are thrust
into the bud vases of their gullets.
The chipmunk crosses in front of me
tail held up like a banner. Who knows
what he has in his cheeks? Beechnuts
would be good, or a morsel of amanita.

Gorki disliked his face with its high
Mongol cheekbones. *It would be good to be*

a bandit, he said, *to rob rich misers*
and give their money to the poor. Saturnine
Gorki, at the 1929 International Congress
of Atheists. By then he was famous, but
twice, in his teens, he tried to kill
himself. Called before an ecclesiastical
tribunal and excommunicated, he declared
God is the name of my desire.

The animals have no Holy Synod to
answer to. They simply pursue their vocations.
In general, I desire to see God lifting
the needy up out of their dung heap,
as it is written. I did not seek this
ancient porcupine curled in the hollow
of a dead ash tree, delicately encoded
on top of a mountain of his own dung,
pale buff-colored pellets that must have
taken several seasons to accumulate.

At this moment, I desire the dogs, oblivious
so far, not to catch sight or scent of him.
I am the rightful master of my soul
Gorki said, and is this not true of the porcupine?
Born Aleksei Maksimovich Peshkov
he chose his own name—*gorki*—bitter
and a century later I carry him
like a pocket guide on this secret trail
clearing and wool-gathering as we go.

Imagining Marianne Moore
in the Butterfly Garden

Surrounded, blundered into by
these gorgeous tropical ephemerae,
we watch their pinwheel colors compose
an arcane calligraphy on air
under a quarter-acre of fine mesh.

I almost step on a slender young botanist
in a shocking-pink smock, lying flat
to pollinate certain recalcitrant flowers
with a single-haired paintbrush.
You bend to inspect her handiwork
your twice-wound braids frizzing red against
the sun to form a sort of web.

Marianne, I was appalled you dared
to chloroform a cat and then
dissect it at Bryn Mawr. Was it
the miniaturist impulse even then,
a schoolgirl's red desire
to see fine things in place?

When our guide uses her second and third
fingers to clasp a palm-sized Heliconid
by one wing, you murmur approvingly,

Precisionist. We peer at the owl eye it wears
as a scare tactic. I see a frisson pierce you
just as the peacocks on the grass at Oxford
once made your hair stand on end, the eyes
of their tail feathers holding you fast.

Worlds apart we are undergraduates
again. Letting the brilliant mimicry
shiver through us.
We are the beasts, you whisper
and I nod, releasing you.
The noiseless Heliconid
soars to another silent flower.

The Greenhouse Effect

Again, look overhead
How air is azurèd. . . .
—THE WORKS OF GERARD MANLEY HOPKINS

The paper in this book was
produced from pure wood pulp without
the use of chlorine or any other
substance harmful to the environment.

I bore it to the indifferent cashier
who could not know that according
to Robert Bridges' introduction
although touchy and arrogant, you
had great sweetness, nor how sweet
it is to replace my lost edition
loaned to a student forty years ago
with this paperback wearing your portrait
as a rosy-lipped boy on the cover.

Dear Gerard, how gentle, how British
the rest of the disclaimer, which ends:
thereby conserving fossil fuels and
contributing little to the greenhouse effect.

Flesh and fleece, fur and feather,
Grass and greenworld all together. . . .
In your lifetime and most of mine, greenhouse
suggested roses out of season,

fleshy gladiolas, even European
cucumbers trained to trellises:

in short, the kind of fervor
that made you burn those early poems for
the love of God, you would have said,
on becoming a Jesuit. For the love
of posterity Bridges saved
most of them, and for the love
of the environment, Wordsworth Editions
reprinted you <u>with ah! bright wings</u>.

Mother of Everyone

MURIEL RUKEYSER 1913–1980

Once a day I lie flat on my back
stretch out the bent sapling of my torso
and raise my four-pound yellow dumbbell.
Working out makes me think of Muriel.
Muriel after her next-to-last stroke
standing a little spraddle-legged for balance
the way I do, although I try to hide
my disequilibrium
by leaning casually against
railings, blackboards, doorjambs.

Passionate Muriel, tough as a tree trunk,
her sure voice containing a vibrato—
had it always been there? I felt it
as a splinter she worked past, line by line
declaiming *surely it is time for the true grace of women* . . .
a young and fervent Muriel evacuated
from Barcelona at the outbreak
of the Spanish civil war on an overcrowded boat
chartered by Belgians when consulates were helpless . . .
obdurate Muriel demanding human rights
for Kim Chi Ha in his Korean cage
a poet in solitary, *glare-lit, I hear,*
without books, without pen or paper

Muriel eulogizing Matty—*Defend us*
from doing what he had to do. . . .
Harvard's F. O. Mattheissen
my favorite professor, who leapt from the closet
out of a Boston hotel window—
and I thought how she was the first woman-poet
I knew who was willing to say the unsaid.

In rehab I was learning how to put one foot
in front of the other, how to lift
a teaspoon from the soup bowl to my lips.
Three months of that. I had
a one-pound weight. They strapped it to my wrist.

In "Resurrection of the Right Side" Muriel tells it:
Word by stammer, walk stammered, the lurching deck of earth.
Who but Muriel, picking her way back
through the earthquake that flattened her, learning
all over again how to smooth a stagger, hold a pen,
enunciate the language she coaxed from her mouth,
who but she could build poems from such rubble.
Muriel, mother of everyone.

Rilke Revisited

Carrying a single
long-stemmed iris
you walk through Prague,
dressed entirely in black,
an uncooked bard whose work,
according to Lou Andreas
Salome, is *florid,*
romantic and obscure.

She makes you change
your name (René at birth),
revise your crabbed longhand,
and put your infantilized
white feet on wet grass.
You work at a stand-up desk
to force the sluggish blood
down to your numb appendages.

You become a vegetarian,
you breakfast on
imported Quaker Oats.
And then come lovers, fans,
translators, your name

on the tongues of literati.
Your angels somersault,
then hover in midair.

I feel them pass by
causing the tips of my hair
to rise crackling
from the sidewise
swipe of their wings.

Pantoum, with Swan

FOR CAROLYN KIZER

Bits of his down under my fingernails
a gob of his spit behind one ear
and a nasty welt where the nib of his beak
bit down as he came. It was our first date.

A gob of his spit behind one ear,
his wings still fanning. I should have known better,
I should have bitten him off on our first date.
And yet for some reason I didn't press charges;

I wiped off the wet. I should have known better.
They gave me the morning-after pill
and shook their heads when I wouldn't press charges.
The yolk that was meant to hatch as Helen

failed to congeal, thanks to the morning-after pill
and dropped harmlessly into the toilet
so that nothing became of the lost yolk, Helen,
Troy, wooden horse, forestalled in one swallow

flushed harmlessly away down the toilet.
The swan had by then stuffed Euripedes, Sophocles
—leaving out Helen, Troy, Agamemnon—
the whole house of Atreus, the rest of Greek tragedy,

. . .

stuffed in my head, every strophe of Sophocles.
His knowledge forced on me, yet Bird kept the power.
What was I to do with ancient Greek history
lodged in my cortex to no avail?

I had his knowledge, I had no power
the year I taught Yeats in a classroom so pale
that a mist enshrouded the ancient religions
and bits of his down flew from under my fingernails.

II

Hard Frost: On a Line by Hopkins

No need now for the newspaper mulch
topped with spoiled hay. It will become
by summer one friable creation.

Irrelevant now the owl balloons at four corners
and the spray made from pulverized seeds
of the neem, revered shade tree of Asia.

The bean plants have fallen to skeletons.
The forgotten tomatoes have imploded
and a black melt has seized the squash vines

but all of the root crops linger, serene in their cubbyholes.
Beets, carrots, parsnips, the tapered white cones known as daikon.
Potatoes still threaded to one another in their labyrinth.

As the Pequots planted fish in their corn hills
I shovel a dead mouse mottled with maggots
hidden how long in a riot of rhubarb leaves

deep down under a barefaced sunflower
deep down for dearest freshness.

Why There Will Always Be Thistle

Sheep will not eat it
nor horses nor cattle
unless they are starving.
Unchecked, it will sprawl over
pasture and meadow
choking the sweet grass
defeating the clover
until you are driven
to take arms against it
but if unthinking
you grasp it barehanded
you will need tweezers
to pick out the stickers.

Outlawed in most Northern
states of the Union
still it jumps borders.
Its taproot runs deeper
than underground rivers
and once it's been severed
by breadknife or shovel
—two popular methods
employed by the desperate—
the bits that remain will

spring up like dragons' teeth
a field full of soldiers
their spines at the ready.

Bright little bursts of
chrome yellow explode from
the thistle in autumn
when goldfinches gorge on
the seeds of its flower.
The ones left uneaten
dry up and pop open
and parachutes carry
their procreant power
to disparate venues
in each hemisphere
which is why there will always
be thistle next year.

The Politics of Bindweed

I have lived all season among the bindweed.
I have spied on their silent Anschluss,
the bugles of their flowers, the dark guy wires
they put down into earth from which to fling
slim vines that burgeon into airy traps.

At eye level I have seen them strangle aster,
milkweed, buttercup; I have taken note of
their seemingly random entanglement by tendril
of the whole drowsy meadow. My own ankles
have been tugged at and held fast by these fanatics.

These barbarian cousins of morning glory
mean to smother the clover, drive out the livestock,
send scouts to infiltrate the next hayfield,
exploit the ties of family and class
until they rule from hedgerow to hedgerow.

Wherefore all season on my hands and knees
I have ripped out roots, stems, ringlets and blossoms.
I have pursued every innocent threadlike structure
to its source, then plucked it. My chosen task is
to reestablish the republic of grasses.

The Brown Mountain

What dies out of us and our creatures,
out of our fields and gardens,
comes slowly back to improve us:
the entire mat of nasturtiums
after frost has blackened them,
sunflower heads the birds
have picked clean, the still
sticky stalks of milkweed
torn from the pasture, coffee grounds,
egg shells, moldy potatoes,
the tough little trees that once
were crowded with brussels sprouts,
tomatoes cat-faced or bitten into
by inquisitive chipmunks,
gargantuan cucumbers gone soft
from repose. Not the corn stalks and shucks,
not windfall apples. These
are sanctified by the horses.
The lettuces are revised
as rabbit pellets, holy with nitrogen.
Whatever fodder is offered the sheep
comes back to us as raisins
of useful dung.

.   .   .

Compost is our future.
The turgid brown mountain
steams, releasing
the devil's own methane vapor,
cooking our castoffs so that from
our spatterings and embarrassments—
cat vomit, macerated mice,
rotten squash, burst berries,
a mare's placenta, failed melons,
dog hair, hoof parings—arises
a rapture of blackest humus.
Dirt to top-dress, dig in. Dirt fit
for the gardens of commoner and king.

The Potato Sermon

Exhumed at the end of the season
from their caverns of love, their loamy
collectives, the little red Norlands
here nibbled at, there split or malformed
turn up in blind budded clusters
smooth-cheeked, delicate, sometimes
surrounding a massive progenitor
while the thick-skinned long-keeping
Kennebecs that at first pretend
to be tree roots or fossils or wrist bones
are rewards for the provident.

You must do this on your knees
switch hitting, with long pauses
closing your eyes as you tunnel
the better to focus on feeling.
The dirt that packs under your fingernails
forms ten grin lines as if you had clawed
through bricks of bitter chocolate.
It's an Easter egg hunt underground.

Once mounded up in the larder
there is starch for the orphan's belly
there is radiant heat for the hungry.

Go forth as if to partake in
night failing, day beginning.
Go forth. The task is simple.
Deliver the warty earth apple.

The Exchange

The neophyte animal psychic
visits my barn at midday.
She is wearing for the occasion
aquamarine eyeliner
a sequined bow in her hair
and a slippery nylon jacket
my gelding loves to explore
with his delicate muzzle.

What do the horses, those thousand-pound
engines of passion and flight,
the horses, long my conspirators,
tell her, who's newly beguiled?
She says the old broodmare knows
how in the other life
I dined abroad with crows
carrion my caviar.

She says the sloe-eyed fillies
know in the next I am meant
no more to eat flesh but simply
to pick grass, switch flies, and roll
as my horses roll after work
thudding down like a wagonload

of watermelons to tip
from side to side on the sand
scratching the struts of their backs.

And yes, I can feel the itch
ascending my spine as we
observe this ritual together
something, she now confesses
she's never witnessed before.
I tell her the ancient Hindus
moved by this scene, inferred
how their gods and demons, while
churning the ocean of milk
in order to make nectar, erred
and out of chaos brought forth
with dished profile, kind eye
and mane woven from many strands of silk
this magnificence, the horse.

Highway Hypothesis

Nothing quite rests the roving eye
like this long view of sloping fields
that rise to a toyshop farmhouse
with matchstick barns and sheds.
A large yellow beetle spits silage
onto an upturned cricket while
several inch-high cars and trucks
flow soundlessly up the spitcurl drive.

Bucophilia, I call it—
nostalgia over a pastoral vista—
where for all I know the farmer
who owns it or rents it just told his
wife he'd kill her if she left him and
she did and he did and now here come
the auctioneer, the serious bidders
and an ant-train of gawking onlookers.

III

Calling Out of Grays Point

They call it a hand-hole, this pit
the size of a child's coffin. In it
Purvis, caked with muck, sweats
trying to solve the tangle
of Bell South's wires and grids.
Fierce with prickers, a jungle
of palmettos surrounds him.

Ever since the day she moved in
she's been without a phone.
The instrument sits mute on
her desk (along with a new translation
of *Introduction to Metaphysics*)
awaiting installation.
                       Purvis
hails from the Ozarks, he isn't one
to mince words. *See what*
some fuckup's gone and done?
Blue-white's sposed to be
tied to blue-white right here, see
how this asshole's got it attached
to red-green? About what I'd expect.
                              · · ·

Heidegger asked, wherein
is the ground of being?
She wonders, given
today's technology
and his gift for introspection
if Heidegger's query, implying
one must suffer to fit in,
would cover these failed connections.

Purvis returns at dawn.
From his tool belt dangle
pliers, wires, screw drivers, bangles
of linked connectors for the lines
still dead. Mice? Moisture?
Crimps in the cable? Trouble-shooter
Purvis vows by day's close
service will be restored.

From his coffin he blasphemes the Lord
loudly (he hadn't guessed
that wire was hot). At sunset
pudgy, garrulous Purvis—it's
hard not to like him—proffers
the gift of his beeper number
packs up his boom box
climbs in his white truck
and departs for a six-pack
and a shower.

. . .

Alone, she tries not
to yield to angst
the inherent emptiness
of a life she cannot call out of.
She misses Purvis, the cream cheese
and bagel she gave
him half of, his hourly harangues
at her door to report how close
he is to success.
But another day
goes down to darkness.

Next morning somebody else—
Eric, who's slender and terse.
Eric, who doesn't make small talk.
Purvis's beeper no longer shrills.
Introvert Heidegger pales.
Businesslike Eric unspools
half a mile of wire, loops it over
the fence, along the sill
of the house, under palmetto cover
and in through her screen.
Jury-rigged but never mind.
Presto! A dial tone!
She never sees Purvis again.

Opening the Doors of Perception
in Grays Point

Louder than panzers
a dozen jets scream overhead.
The knife edge of solitude
presses against her throat.
Displaced, a paying guest

she slides back the doors
of the bathhouse to let in
the staghorn ferns, the dry
chitter of palm leaves
the black blight on the roses.

Chlorine lilts from the turquoise pool.
She puts her winter self in a chaise longue
under the kind sun. Leisure
is sticky. Thirst troubles her
like an unanswered letter.

Soundlessly at dusk the cats arrive.
Over the rooftop, over the fence's
iron palings, the padlocked gates
to take up their stations in pools of black.
Under a table, behind a flower pot.

. . .

The cats jitter and box in the dark.
Sleepless she dials and redials
her memory call service.
These must be hers, the calm syllables
that speak her name on command.

All night long planes
crisscross the patio streaking
toward London or Rome.
In time she will learn to sleep
through their raw music.

8 A.M. in Grays Point

At the bloody crossroads of narrative and culture
to quote Matthew Arnold, she goes out for her
morning power walk around the perimeter.
Others are doggedly working out: the smiling
bald man with headphones, two sleek older women
not quite as leathery as she but pumping
their elbows as she does, and glistening
with her sweat. One poor soul stubbing along
on her four-prong aluminum crutch, and a young
dog walker enmeshed in several leashes.

Despite the rush hour traffic at the bloody
crossroads beyond the high stucco wall, she
knows she has entered Paradise.
The people who live here are doctors and lawyers
who carefully space their children
eat from the five food groups, endorse
ballet and theater. Their foreign cars
are waxed and polished. Their lives are guarded
by speed bumps. Sprayed with poisons, their lawns
wear discreet little Danger signs.

At the crossroads the 8 o'clock bus disgorges the maids
languidly moving toward their employment.

They carry string bags, they walk, when they can, in the shade,
in sandals or old shoes with cutouts for bunions.
They are not for the most part Anglo, or thin,
these Marias. Even the young ones look old.
By rote to the voice of the vacuum, the swish of the wet mop
all day they will jiggle and waltz on broad hips
the babies and toddlers who reach up to be held.
Without them, Paradise would teeter and fall.

Afoot in Grays Point

Without a single peep-hole
through the crimson blare
of bougainvillea, she jogs
the empty streets, voyeur

peering down private drives
through iron gates, to keep
secret watch how heavily
the freighted houses sleep

and as the day grows brighter
how cobalt blue the bins
curbside for cardboard, plastic jugs
junk mail, newsprint, and cans

how jauntily Green Meadows
Landscape Care, three palms
a freehand frieze on the panel truck
shatters the sunrise calm.

How Zephyr Hills thereafter
succeeds the mowers' pother
hiking natural spring water from
one shoulder to the other

         .   .   .

Miami Rescue Mission
following close behind
to suck up a scuttled desk beside
a television gone blind

in which she sees reflected
a bank of cumuli
which shift as she approaches, while
a single dove nearby

tests the newly sheared
and pesticided lawn
then breasts the stuccoed wall that keeps
the golden people in.

My Life

WITH THREE LINES CULLED FROM HENRY VAUGHAN

While my life is taking place
in four rented pink and green rooms
where faux purple grapes adorn a table lamp
at dusk a cruise ship as long as a city block
and seven storeys high outside my window
is nudged to sea by tugboats, trumpets, and fireworks
and on an adjoining pier a cargo container
disgorges twenty dehydrated humans
along with three corpses.

While my life is taking place
a televangelist explains from a drop-down set
in the fluorescent kitchen how heaven
is shaping up to be a seamless silver city filled
with Vaughan's bright *shootes* of everlastingnesse.

I am smashing bright shoots of garlic when
my parents waft past on the highway
the dead travel while my here-and-now fingers
are picking up and putting down knives, vinegar;
while my fingers and forehead are rebraiding
bright shoots, dream wisps arrive from my past
all gone into the world of light! namely, a long line
of waif dogs; the starveling mare I rescued

who never learned to love me but abided
safely and aloof; my three departed die-hard
brothers still estranged; and now the police are called
to round up a dozen straying illegals
who swam ashore from cigarette boats beaching
amid the suntans and volleyball of snowbirds.

O wasteful heaven, the Jewel of the Just!
Placeless heaven full
of disorderly remembrance, come,
come in while my life is taking place.

IV

Ghazal: On the Table

I was taught to smooth the aura at the end,
said my masseuse, hands hovering at the end.

Inches above my placid pummeled self
did I feel something floating at the end?

Or is my naked body merely prone
to ectoplasmic vapors to no end?

Many other arthritics have lain here
seeking to roll pain's boulder end on end.

Herbal oils, a CD playing soft
loon calls, wave laps, bird trills now must end.

I rise and dress, restored to lift and bend,
my ethereal wisp invisible at the end.

Wagons

Their wheelchairs are Conestoga wagons drawn
into the arc of a circle at 2 P.M.

Elsie, Gladys, Hazel, Fanny, Dora
whose names were coinage after the First World War

remember their parents tuned to the Fireside Chats,
remember in school being taught to hate the Japs.

They sit attentive as seals awaiting their fish
as the therapist sings out her cheerful directives:

Square the shoulders, lean back, straighten the knee
and lift! Tighten, lift and hold, Ladies!

They will retrain the side all but lost in a stroke,
the spinal cord mashed but not severed in traffic.

They will learn to adjust to their newly replaced
hips, they will walk on feet of shapely plastic.

This darling child in charge of their destiny
will lead them forward across the prairie.

The Woman Who Moans

is not in pain.
She is making the sounds
of speech. She drums
her heels, a child strapped
against her will
in the stroller. Perhaps
she protests, perhaps
she agrees in full
with the therapists
when they wheel her chair
to the standing table
and fasten her legs
to supports that brace
her upright. See how
she clings to the tabletop?
Whether she begs
or resists release
is hard to tell
from the song she sings,
moans that ascend
to a blackbird's warble.

Eventually,
restrained like a pup

on a leash, she will learn
once again to walk.
One on each side
they will hold her up
by her voyaging belt
but the sounds she emits
will not change. The fault-
line in her brain
will continue to gape
and the bus, the Forty-
second Street bus
that caught her midstep
and hurled her aloft
will go on transporting
the rest of us.

Grady, Who Lost a Leg in Korea, Addresses Me in the Rehab Gym

He fondles the stump.
See these here flaps along the seam?
Dog ears, they're called.
Gotta work em down
like pie dough with a roller pin
get em smooth enough to set against
the fiberglass. It's light as eggshell.
Gwan, try my leg. Pick it up.

Never could wear the one
they fit me to at the V.A.
Mostly metal, weighed a ton
to cart around, but now—
nodding at another amputee
practicing between
the parallel bars—*I'm gonna*
give it another try.

Grady calls me Parrot Head
—the metal cage that holds
my broken neck—I call him Ahab.
Even though we're little more
than fellow inmates in
the neuro unit on the topmost floor

down here we're life companions
makin a game of it.

Now those guys over there
in chairs? They got the sugar.
Diabetes. Works like a cannibal,
one leg, then the other.
Toes first, foot next, then the knee.
And when they got no other way
to stop the rot, they saw
the goddamn leg off up to here.

He draws his hand across his groin.
Can't fit a thing to that.
You gotta have a stump.
They call em double amputees.
You see em outside on good days
doin wheelies, rearin back
to jump the sidewalk curb
like a bunch of acrobats

makin a game of it.
And once I get the hang of this
I'm gonna waltz my way around
the gym. And then
I'm gonna ask you, Parrot Head,
Wanna dance?

Grand Canyon

Past the signs that say *Stop! Go Back!*
We Are Friendly Indians! past the tables
of garnet and red rock, of turquoise and silver,
past horses thin as paper, profiled
against a treeless horizon, I come
to where all roads converge, I stand
at each of a dozen jumping-off places
with my fellow cripples, my fellow Americans
peering into our national abyss.

Outings for wheelchair postulants
are regular affairs here on the brink
of this improbable upheaved landscape;
the clinic for chronic pain my therapists
back East referred me to is,
by Western measurements, just down the road.
The group is quiet. Wind music lobs
endless songs to would-be suicides
from the river bottom's Loreleis,
a redemptive eight-hour hike below us,
but no one's leapt this week. Some travel
both ways on the bony backs of mules,
slaves forever on this tortuous trail.

.   .   .

Despite the crowds, despite the kitsch,
this mesa, this elevated plain
has always been on my life list.
Life-list, a compound noun in my
directory. The fact is, I'm alive.
The fact is, no conjecture can resolve
why I survived this broken neck
known in the trade as the hangman's fracture,
this punctured lung, eleven broken ribs,
a bruised liver, and more. Enslaved

three months in axial traction, in what they call
a halo, though stooped, I'm up. I'm vertical.
How to define chronic pain?
Maddening, unremitting,
raying out from my spinal cord
like the arms of an octopus, squeezing,
insidious as the tropic anaconda. . . .
The experts are fond of saying
spinal cord injuries are like
snowflakes; no two are ever the same
but while you're lying on the table, unfrocked
—no one tells you this—the twists and pummels,
the stretches and presses are identical.
One size of therapy fits all.

Who practices for disaster? Who
anticipates that the prized horse will bolt,
that you will die/should have/didn't?

That a year will pass before
you can walk the line they ask a drunk to,
or balance on one foot. Who knew
the dumb left hand could be retrained
to cut meat, brush teeth, and yet the day I signed
my name in loose spaghetti loops beneath
the intended line, I wept. We joked
I'd buy a stamp pad, roll my thumb,
some day receive outrageous sums
from Sotheby's for my auctioned print,
brave banter we all but choked
on, but better than the cant that says,
be grateful you're alive, thank God.
Implicit in it, *you've had it too good.*

What would the friendly Indians trade
to break loose from the white man who
reduced them to servitude?
What would the suicidal barter
for deliverance from
the Sisyphean boulder
they daily roll uphill?
What would I trade to regain
my life the way it was?
From pillar to abyss
the answer echoes still:
The word is *everything.*

V

William Remembers the Outbreak of Civil War
1983

I took off my clothes and walked naked. There were
people killing boys just for their clothes.

I walked with the rest of my Dinka clan
a thousand kilometers, single file.

We blistered our feet in the desert dirt
the flyaway dirt of southern Sudan.

If my mother sat down beside me today
I wouldn't know her. My father was one

of the elders who put us out on the march
with our cooking pots and killing sticks

before he got ready to shake hands with death
in the war, the war that was always coming.

I was too little to carry a dang—
a pole with a hand grip, carved out of tree roots—

Khartoumers made fun of us, calling us stupid
stick-people, Tagbondo. *All that was long ago.*

                          . . .

I was six years old. I had only a shirt.
Lots of us dropped out along the way

recruited to join guerrilla bands,
given machetes, beer, even guns.

The oldest, sixteen. In the refugee camp
in Kakuma I learned English, team sports

shower and soap, fork and spoon.
I studied geography, read Lord Jim

and coached younger boys in basketball
a game made for Dinkas. Even skinny and homesick

we're the tallest tribe in the world, it is written.
The war never ended, the camp overflowed.

Some people from the UN came to see
the city of lost boys lodged in this settlement.

One of them sent me a pair of Nikes.
Nikes, my first shoes. The day those shoes came

I was King, let me tell you. King of the camp.

———

Framed against buildings, in gray suit-and-tie
tall handsome William, who's birthdayless

. . .

but guesses he's twenty-two or -three
a shipping clerk now in the Western world

says, *Truly my whole life I never knew*
where I would put my head down at night

what I would eat, what day I would eat it
what day my head would drop off my shoulders.

Now I am at my highest place yet.
I sleep without fear. I eat without hoarding

but I worry about all the other boys
of the Dinka clan I left behind

in the Kakuma camp with their useless dangs
and their cooking pots and no relatives

no kin to turn to as long as they live.

Identifying the Disappeared

The exiles have returned from safe cold places
with their resistance to forgetting, returned
with brush and spoon, sieve and dustpan
to bring back the bones of a child, which are become
the bones of a nesting bird; the lip of a clavicle
transformed into angel wings which want to be
its mother; skulls for uncle, father, brother
who soiled themselves and died in the Resistance.

It is another day to walk about
testing the earth for springy places to insert
their tools, another day to see what the dead
saw in that instant after the machete
severed the critical artery,
after the eye went milky and the soul
flew away in horror and the flesh retreated
in narrow strips, like ribbons, from the bone.

The exiles have come back. They are breaking
the sleep of earth, they are packing the dry shards
of the disappeared in cardboard cartons
Relief provides—wood is scarce here—

and still they store up the names of the murderers
who have put away their uniforms and persuasions
under the landmine of respectability,
the trigger, God willing, one day they will trip on.

Bringing Down the Birds

FOR CHRISTOPHER COKINOS

Does it make you wince to hear
how the last of the world's great auks
were scalded to death on the Newfoundland coast
in vats of boiling water so that
birdshot would not mutilate the feathers
that stuffed the mattress your great-grandparents
lay upon, begetting your forebears?

Are you uncomfortable reading how
the flocks of passenger pigeons
that closed over the sky like an eyelid
the millions that roared like thunder
like trains, like tornados were wiped out, expunged
in a free-for-all a hundred years gone?
Can you bear the metaphor in how it was done?

Pet pigeons, their eyelids sewn, were tied
to stools a few feet off the ground until
hordes of their kind swooped overhead.
Released, their downward flutter lured
the multitude who were smothered in nets

while trappers leaped among them
snapping their necks with pincers.
The feathers from fifty pigeons
added up to a pound of bedding.

Does it help to name the one-or-two-of-a-kind
Martha or Rollie and exhibit them in a zoo
a kindly zoo with moats in place of wire
or clone from fished-up bits of DNA
a creature rather like the creature
it had been, left to the whim of nature?

Would bringing the ivory bill back from deep woods
to a greenhouse earth placate the gods?
The harlequin-patterned Labrador duck
the dowdy heath hen, the gregarious Carolina parakeet
that once bloomed like daffodils in flight,
if science could reconstruct them, how long
would it take us logging and drilling and storing up
treasures to do them all in again?

Soldiers

Old-timers itchy from waiting for
the three-toed sloth to wake and turn their way,
sweaty from hiking with binoculars
and camera to glimpse the reclusive quetzal,

stiff-legged on the trail of the wattled bell bird,
the anteater, the boa constrictor, begin
under the eyes of their Costa Rican guide
to exchange the massive data of their days.

The beaches they stormed at Normandy,
Anzio, Saipan refill with flak
and thudding shells. One of them ferried
ordnance over the Burmese Hump.

Another lay fathoms deep in a submarine
under arctic ice. One, culled from the infantry,
was shipped to Los Alamos to begin
the secret life that led (shame mixed with pride)

to the Bomb. Called at last to attention
they stargaze to see, under the guide's supervision,
a termite tunnel that rises above their heads
to a bulbous nest alive with pale-bodied clones.

.   .   .

When birds peck a hole in the passage, the rosy-cheeked
chief biologist explains, one
of the soldier termites, rudely bitter to taste,
offers his head for the good of the tribe within

as these old soldiers did, though how many classmates
equally clever with rifle and swift with grenade pin
nevertheless were left among the dead.
Weary heroes, they dream themselves back

in the perilous nest of the last good war
and wake at dawn to the birds' territorial shrieks
they are pleased to interpret as music.

Capital Punishment

On the way to his death Benny Demps
complained about what had happened
backstage: when they couldn't raise a vein
in either arm they went to his groin
which also refused to yield and then
cut his leg open. It was bloody
said the 10 o'clock news on TV
but they finally made connection.

We are shown only the flat
uninhabited metal stretcher
but as the black curtain oozed upward
Benny went on calling for justice
from his tidy blue-sheeted gurney
demanding an investigation
into the pain they had caused him
the botch they had made of his exit.

Now we are given pictures
of victims in Sierra Leone.
The thing about the machete
is how quickly bone and gristle
will dull it, how often
you have to sit down and hone it

to hack off those hundreds of limbs
above or below the elbow.

One village elder was spared his thumbs.
On camera he holds out his arms
to show us what you can do
with two thumbs. Some
of the armless dripping blood
ran into the bush after their attackers
crying, *come back, I implore you!*
Come back and kill us, please kill us.

The newscast goes blank. Silver
streaks jitter across the screen
which finally fills with merciful snow.
Why are we shown mutilations
and denied execution? I long
to go back and hear out Benny Demps
taxing this vengeful world of slash
and burn and inject, I want

to be there for the last act
in his ruthless life, the scene
we were not permitted to witness,
his naïve six-minute diatribe
against the state, the vitriol
of his soliloquy running down
like a windup toy:
the gentleness of his exit.

Want

The world is awash in unwanted dogs:
look-alike yellow curly-tailed mongrels that come
collared and wormed, neutered and named, through customs
come immunized, racketing and rabies-tagged

to Midwestern farms from Save the Children, the Peace Corps
come from Oxfam into the carpeted bedrooms of embassies
into the Brooklyn lofts of CARE workers on leave
the London, Paris, Geneva homes of Doctors Without Borders

and still the streets of Asmara, Kigali, Bombay
refill with ur-dogs: those bred-back scavenging flea-ridden
sprung-ribbed bitches whose empty teats make known
the latest bitten-off litter of curs that go back to the Pleistocene.

And what of the big-headed stick-figured children naked
in the doorways of Goma, Luanda, Juba, Les Hants
or crouched in the dust of haphazard donkey-width tracks
that connect the named and the nameless hamlets of Want?

There will always be those who speed past unbeguiled.
There will always be somewhere a quorum of holy fools
who wade into the roiling sea despite the tsunami
to dip teaspoon after teaspoon from the ocean.

VI

The Long Marriage

The sweet jazz
of their college days
spools over them
where they lie
on the dark lake
of night growing
old unevenly:
the sexual thrill
of Peewee Russell's
clarinet; Jack
Teagarden's trombone
half syrup, half
sobbing slide;
Erroll Garner's
rusty hum-along
over the ivories;
and Glenn Miller's
plane going down
again before sleep
repossesses them . . .

Torschlusspanik.
Of course
the Germans have

a word for it,
the shutting of
the door,
the bowels' terror
that one will go
before
the other as
the clattering horse
hooves near.

Keeping in Touch

Either a series of minor earthquakes or
the weekly announcement of another
paroled rapist offsets the clement weather,

mimosas loosing showers of yellow pollen,
the worst of a series of offending allergens
in this graduate student cinderblock warren

where pipes burst and playgrounds overflow
and every aspiring Asian family makes do.
Three black-eyed toddlers under my window

trill back and forth in their mother tongue
scolding dolls they pick up and rock and abandon,
shake them, forgive them, rerock and put down

mornings when you call me long distance to report
it is 5 below in English and Fahrenheit
in New Hampshire, and I remember my high school part

in Thornton Wilder's one-act, "The Happy Journey
from Trenton to Camden"—thirty miles by early
auto—staged with wooden chairs to signify

. . .

the family coupe that sported running boards
as now 3,000 miles apart we prop our words
in place of touch, dial, redial, and hoard

absence with its pucker of California citrus
that comes between and yet keeps us.

Hark, Hark

The phones, the long-distance phones are ringing.
The satellite phone from the field camp in Kosovo.
The lawyer's phone in a complex in Palo Alto.
The car phone conveying a child to baseball practice.
In this way the siblings converse and condole

much as the now-vanished Carolina parakeets
with their sunflower-yellow heads
and kindergarten-green backs
swooped down to their captured kin
and fluttered all night in noisy flocks
against the cage, their opposing breasts
marked with the wire grids that kept them apart
until the last ornamental bird was extinguished

as we will be, but not without having first
listened in to the ongoing shrill, with all of its
anxieties and triumphs taking place among
the offspring we raised, pre-analog transmission
and the ones they are raising in a cacophony of connection.

The Joy of Cooking, 1931

In my smudge-thumbed
first edition

Irma Rombauer
says *It is*

a thrill to possess
shelves well stocked

with home-canned food.
Agreed.

And so we've picked
twenty pounds

of high fox grapes
twined around

a treed escarp
and lugged the pail

home, uphill.
In fact, she avers

. . .

you will find
their inspection

—often sur-
reptitious—

(The fat blue-bot-
tomed pot begins

to spit and pop.
It smells delicious.)

and the pleasure
of serving the fruit

of your labor
(I mash the burst

globes, let simmer.
The season cambers

toward winter.
Strain juice, measure,

reboil with sugar.
Upend jars

on covered table.)
comparable

. . .

only to a clear
conscience. Dear

Mrs. Rombauer,
time takes us singly

and ungently
down the jellied

slope to here.
When we're gone,

let sunlight shine
through jars and jars.

Wood

Every November we buy from the logger
a cord of trash wood, the green tops of weedy poplar
for the horses to gnaw on all winter, studiously stripping
the bark in long, juicy curls, thereby sparing
our fence boards from the deep curves
seen elsewhere on poor-mouth farms.
And then it is spring.
                    Dr. Green arrives
rich with dandelions, bromegrass, and clover.
The six-foot spindles of now-naked popples clutter
the paddock, the lawn, the roadside. You insist
they must be gathered and stacked to be sawn.
Someone can burn them, they make a quick fire.
As quick as newspaper, I say. I want to hurl them
into the gully. Let nature do the recycling.

Of course you win. After living so long a time
side by side, I know how to choose; what quarrels
not to pick.
                And so in the chartreuse days
of April we work together stacking by size
neat piles of trash wood to gladden the eye:
wood enough for the hereafter.

Domesticity

Oh, what a weak sticker, you groan, as the batter pops
out to the infield. We're propped
up in two beds—mine's electric, with crib
sides, rented to ease eleven broken ribs—
watching the Red Sox, who are in the cellar
and dozing between Demerol and errors.

You yawn, the resident optimist
no family should lack, always stitching
a selvedge along the silver lining
—the luck of my unbroken pelvis—
so that when in a bizarre twist
they tie it up in the bottom of the ninth
you crow, they're still alive and kicking!
We rouse as for the crisis of an old friend
and watch through extra innings to the end.

John Green Takes His Warner, New Hampshire, Neighbor to a Red Sox Game

Everett down the hill's
52 and trim. No beer gut.
Raises beef, corn, hay, cuts
cordwood between harvests.
Goes to bed at 8 and falls
into sleep like a parachutist.

He's never been to a ballgame.
He's never been to Boston though
he went over to Portland Maine
one time ten, fifteen years ago.

In Sullivan Square, they
luck out, find a space
for John's car, take
the T to Fenway Park.
The famous T!
A kind of underground trolley.
Runs in the dark.
No motorman that Ev can see.
Jammed with other sports fans.

John has to show him
how to put the token in.

How to press with his hips
to go through the turnstile.
How to stand back while
the doors whoosh shut.
How to grab a strap
as the car pitches forward.
How to push out
with the surging crowd.

Afterward Ev says the game's
a whole lot better on tv.
Too many fans.
Too many other folks for him.

Lying in Bed Away from Home

Cardinals outside this window ask *cheer what cheer*
as they did from childhood's oaks, their voices smeared

with Latin unguents from the Sisters of St. Joseph's
Mass next door till the fire station's braying riffs

and hoots uphill raised my father from his chair
to pursue the immense arsons of his desire

my unemployed uncles up front in the bile-green Packard
my teenage brothers asprawl in the back, and I anchored

at the window overlooking Carpenter Lane
as the hook-and-ladder flew past with all my male kin

giving chase as if to extract some mysterious essence
from the sorrows of those burned out or down for insurance.

What did I know, sent early to bed, girlchild
parched with my own small longings, how it was to thrill

to the luck of escape from the flames, to the whiff of sex
the siren gave off that sang them away from the redbirds' nest.

A Place by the Sea

. . . bottomless perdition, there
   to dwell.
   —JOHN MILTON

Now there is nothing, my father said, mock-groaning
as he wrote out the check for his taxes, between me
and a word I heard as Perdistant, a place possibly
next door to Atlantic City, that playground of sand and sins,
private nudist beaches, and even then, slot machines.

And did he arrive there, my father, after his third and final
heart attack, the EMTs pounding his chest
shouting Pete, Pete, come back, twirling the dials,
trying to jump-start his paltry machine with theirs?

And was it what I had pictured, the broadest and best
of vistas, when I the apprentice tried to decipher
the code of my parent, his hapless what-the-hell shrug
in the face of Perdistant, I his five-year-old daughter
climbing the tree of his torso to partake of his hug?

Flying

When Mother was little, all
that she knew about flying was what
her bearded grandfather told her:
every night your soul flies
out of your body and into
God's lap. He keeps it under
his handkerchief until morning.

Hearing this as a child haunted me.
I couldn't help sleeping.
I woke up each morning groping
as for a lost object lodged perhaps
between my legs, never knowing
what had been taken from me or what
had been returned to its harbor.

When as a new grandmother
my mother first flew cross-country
—the name of the airline escapes me
but the year was 1947—
she consigned her soul to the Coco-
Chanel-costumed stewardess
then ordered a straight-up martini.

· · ·

As they landed, the nose wheel wobbled
and dropped away. Some people screamed.
My mother was not one of them
but her shoes—she had slipped them off—
somersaulted forward. Deplaning
she took out her handkerchief
and reclaimed her soul from the ashen stewardess.

That night in a room not her own
under eaves heavy with rain
and the rue of a disbelieving daughter
my mother described her grandfather to me
a passionate man who carried his soul
wedged deep in his pants' watch-pocket:
a pious man whose red beard had never seen scissors

who planted his carrots and beets
in the dark of the moon for good reason
and who, before I was born,
rose up like Elijah.
Flew straightaway up into heaven.

Giving Birth

FOR YANN, AT NINETEEN

Every month I went to the obstetrician. The sign
over his examining table said: Familiarity
Breeds. Every month I lay down on the hard slab
to be poked and peered at, or—this was before ultrasound—
palpated per rectum. Every month I answered
the same perfunctory questions:
any trouble with our waterworks? Are we sleeping?
Every month I was ushered out by Dr. Congeniality
as if this were indeed a joint enterprise
and not the singular journey I took three times.

No father was permitted to attend.
No mother to be conscious during the crossing.
Painkillers and truth serums were the drugs of choice.
I thrashed and swore furiously, I was told, ex post facto.
My vocabulary astonished the interns.
Thus Demeroled and scopolamined, my body
slammed through the waves without me
only taking me back in when a face
leaned over mine each time in the recovery room
and said, Congratulations. You have a girl.
You have a girl. You have a boy.

· · ·

Even after landfall I was held in bed.
During the week-long stay in Maternity no infant
could cross the threshold of the four-mothers-to-a-room
except at feeding time. The medley
of sobbing babies being trundled up and down
the corridor at 6-10-2-6-10
swelled and subsided, tragic doppler music

so that when your mother nineteen years ago
asked me to be her birth partner, I swelled
with prestige. I went to birthing classes
for the breathing, the panting, the back rubs.
I packed special teas and lotions.
Ever efficient, she went into labor before my plane
had touched down on the far side of the Atlantic.

Darkness drifted on us from the mountains.
We drove to the hospital pausing between contractions.
The midwives—one spoke German,
the other, French—installed us in a bedroom
wallpapered with nosegays of roses.
No metal crib sides. No stirrups. Everyone
was eerily cheerful. The boyish doctor
strode in still clutching his motorcycle helmet
seemingly uneasy in this gathering of women,
content to be a bit player unless needed.

Painfully and with enormous effort your mother opened.
Mottled purple and black-haired, an unexpected

animal emerged from the tunnel. I gasped.
The midwives handed me this hard foreign muscle
that flexed and contracted from the shock of entry.
I held it in a shallow basin of warm water
and sloshed it with antiseptic soap to remove
the coating it had come with and then carried it
to the bed where it magicked into the baby
your mother had brought forth and now put to her breast.

You slept in the curl of your mother's body
as we four women drank champagne
and ate zweibach and congratulated each other.
At first light, driving your mother's little Renault
I followed the German-speaking midwife
back through the unfamiliar streets
back to the converted farmhouse overlooking
the border crossing where we honked farewells
and the sun came up unsurprised.

A Game of Nettles

Torture, we called it, stripped to the waist
three girl cousins nine and ten
who'd learned a light caress would break
the leaf tip sac and sting the skin

like summer's dreaded typhoid shots.
Whoever let go first was Out
and each of us contrived to lose
in the back fields of innocence

entire mornings in July.
We stroked the dark green hairy leaves
across our chests to feel the fuse
ignite our pale mysterious disks.

Tinctured with uneasiness
our nipples startled and leapt up.
Called in to lunch, washed, combed and dressed
we sat at table, little beasts

secretly burning inside our shirts
not knowing we had stumbled on
forbidden pleasures, adult sport,
not knowing we were masochists.

The Collection

In Gestapo-ridden Paris, Bertrand,
a boy I met once he was safe in Queens,
cruised the Metro nightly with a razor
blade concealed between his fingers
for harvesting sundry decorations
from the chests of sodden German soldiers.

Only child, too young to be a courier
in the Resistance, he spent the year he should
have been bar mitzvahed slept against,
felt up, and vomited on. He loved geometry
even then, at home in three dimensions,
grew up to be an astrophysicist.

No drama in the rest of Bertrand's life
spent measuring black holes, red giants,
could match the terror in the slither
of his fingers, the thrill of slicing
trophies from their moorings, then pocketing
the stash to add to his collection.

He brought it to the States in bonbon boxes,
one for ribbons and tinny iron crosses,
the other for thickly tarnished buttons,

and kept them in a knapsack under his bed.
High school seniors, we clung to each other
while his parents divorced, that year in Queens

but when I spent the night in Bertrand's bed
he unpacked and fondled his treasures
as if I were no longer there.

The Angel

You didn't have to be a Catholic mother
to march with the Catholic Mothers Against The War
and lie in front of the Navy Yard buses waiting

to ferry recruits to their berths in Boston Harbor.
You didn't have to be any kind of mother.
One was a priest, two others merely fathers.

You didn't have to have a war resister—
my 17-year-old son—to serve as adviser.
Arrested twice for civil disobedience,

he knew the holding pen they put us in,
30 middle-class and mostly Catholic women.
He stood up with his father and the bondsman.

The whole world was watching. Nothing I could
have done back then in self-righteousness
would have impeded my body's downward slippage.

I am too old now to go to jail for my conscience,
to wait to be processed, dismissed with a click
of the stapler. These days I take them by the hand,

.   .   .

each woman I walk to the door of the clinic
past the chants of *Murderer! Baby killer!* Who are
the harassers? My old compatriots' granddaughters?

What a long purgatory life is,
a tethered dog on the lawn next door forever
struggling against the circle he carves for himself,

wearing his claws to stubs in the hard pack,
awaiting the angel he summons with his bark,
the angel who comes at last to unfasten his collar.

VII

The Ancient Lady Poets

I, who alone survived, move through
my old age like a camera
in the hands of a hard-core realist
bending over knucklebones on the lawn
or the rot of a long-dead red squirrel
after the snow has melted.

The landscape of my body up close
is one of snags and glaciations.
You can see the path of a forest fire
that devoured one breast leaving
the other shyly hanging in space,
my still abundant hair whitening,
my almost bald pubis still useful.

We had planned to age elegantly.
The Japanese twins who lived to
one hundred and seven could not have
outdone us cruising Fifth Avenue in
our custom-made shoes, our handsome
obedient Dalmatians heeling beside us.

· · ·

Hatless, earringed, no sign of scoliosis
we'd planned to stride forth block
after block, well-published, polished.

Bad girls of the New England Poetry Club
our wit and fame up ahead
leading a procession of disciples.

Three Dreams After a Suicide

—ANNE SEXTON, 1974

1.

We're gathered in the funeral home, your friends
who are not themselves especially friends,
with you laid out on view in the approved fashion
wearing the bright-red reading dress with cut-glass buttons
that wink at the ceiling, when you spring
like a jack-in-the-box from the coffin
crying Boo! I was only fooling!

2.

After the terrible whipping you are
oddly pleased with yourself,
an impenitent child, the winner.
It's Daddy Death who's quit.
Once more you've worn him out
from all his lifting and striking.
His belt lies shredded in his meaty fist.

3.

We are standing together in a sunless garden
in Rockport, Mass. I'm wearing the hat
the artist painted you in

and suddenly swarms of wasps
fly up under the downturned brim.

O death, where is thy sting?
Tar baby, it is stickered to me; you
were my wasp and I your jew.

Oblivion

The dozen ways they did it—
off a bridge, the back of a boat,
pills, head in the oven, or
wrapped in her mother's old mink coat
in the garage, a brick on the accelerator,
the Cougar's motor thrumming
while she crossed over.

What they left behind—
the outline of a stalled novel, diaries,
their best poems, the note that ends
now will you believe me,
offspring of various ages, spouses
who cared and weep and yet
admit relief now that it's over.

How they fester, the old details
held to the light like a stained-glass icon
—the shotgun in the mouth, the string
from toe to trigger; the tongue
a blue plum forced between his lips
when he hanged himself in her closet—
for us it is never over

. . .

who raced to the scene, cut the noose,
pulled the bathtub plug on pink water,
broke windows, turned off the gas,
rode in the ambulance, only minutes later
to take the body blow of bad news.
We are trapped in the plot, every one.
Left behind, there is no oblivion.

Acknowledgments

Some of these poems have appeared, sometimes in slightly differ-
ent form or under different titles, in the following publications:

Agni: "Capital Punishment," "William Remembers the Outbreak
of Civil War"

Arts & Letters: "8 A.M. in Grays Point," "Opening the Doors
of Perception in Grays Point," "The Woman Who Moans"

The Atlantic Monthly: "Oblivion"

The Boston Book Review: "Why There Will Always Be Thistle"

The Connecticut Review: "Flying," "Grady, Who Lost a Leg in Korea,
Addresses Me in the Rehab Gym"

Country Journal: "Wood"

Epoch: "Soldiers," "The Ancient Lady Poets"

Five Points: "Grand Canyon," "The Greenhouse Effect," "Identifying
the Disappeared"

The Georgia Review: "Bringing Down the Birds," "Hard Frost: On
a Line by Hopkins," "Imagining Marianne Moore in the Butterfly
Garden," "*The Joy of Cooking*, 1931," "Mother of Everyone,"
"My Life," "Want"

The Hudson Review: "Skinnydipping with William Wordsworth"

Kalliope: "A Game of Nettles"

The Maine Times: "Highway Hypothesis"

The Massachusetts Review: "The Exchange"

The Michigan Quarterly Review: "The Angel," "The Collection"

The New Yorker: "Ghazal: On the Table," which appeared as
"On the Table," "Three Dreams After a Suicide"

Nightsun: "Domesticity"

Orbis (England): "A Place by the Sea"

Ploughshares: "Thinking of Gorki While Clearing a Trail," "Hark, Hark"
Poetry: "Lying in Bed Away from Home"
Poetry International: "Afoot in Grays Point," "Calling Out of Grays Point"
The Progressive: "The Politics of Bindweed," which appeared as "Poem for an Election Year: The Politics of Bindweed"
River City: "The Potato Sermon"
Washington Square: "Rilke Revisited"
Witness: "The Brown Mountain," "Pantoum, with Swan"

I am indebted to Bernard F. Scholz, Professor of Comparative Literature, Rijks Universiteit, Groningen, Netherlands, for providing the derivation of the word *torschlusspanik*: it "refers to the rush in and out just before the city gates were closed in the walled towns of the principalities which dotted Germany until Napoleon put an end to the 'Kleinstaaterei.'"

The late Anne Sexton wrote the phrase "Muriel, mother of everyone" in thanking Muriel Rukeyser for sending her a copy of *The Speed of Darkness*.